COOL
CONSTRUCTION
& BUILDING BLOCKS
CRAFTING CREATIVE TOYS & AMAZING GAMES

**REBECCA
FELIX**

Checkerboard
Library

An Imprint of Abdo Publishing
abdopublishing.com

ABDOPUBLISHING.COM

Published by Abdo Publishing, a division of ABDO, PO Box 398166, Minneapolis, Minnesota 55439. Copyright © 2016 by Abdo Consulting Group, Inc. International copyrights reserved in all countries. No part of this book may be reproduced in any form without written permission from the publisher. Checkerboard Library™ is a trademark and logo of Abdo Publishing.

Printed in the United States of America, North Mankato, Minnesota

102015
012016

THIS BOOK CONTAINS
RECYCLED MATERIALS

Content Developer: Nancy Tuminelly
Design and Production: Mighty Media, Inc.
Editor: Liz Salzmann
Photo Credits: cjmacer/Shutterstock, David Wilson/Flickr, Levent Konuk/ Shutterstock, Mighty Media, Inc., Shutterstock, Simone Mescolini/Shutterstock

The following manufacturers/names appearing in this book are trademarks:
Craft Smart®, Crayola®, EasyCast®, LEGO®, LINCOLN LOGS®, Sharpie®

Library of Congress Cataloging-in-Publication Data
Felix, Rebecca, 1984- author.
  Cool construction & building blocks : crafting creative toys & amazing games / by Rebecca Felix.
     pages cm. -- (Cool toys & games)
  Includes index.
  ISBN 978-1-68078-047-5
1. LEGO toys--Juvenile literature. 2. Blocks (Toys)--Juvenile literature. 3. Models and modelmaking--Juvenile literature. I. Title. II. Title: Cool construction and building blocks.
  TS2301.T7 F375
  688.7'2--dc23
                          2015033042

CONTENTS

BRICKS, BLOCKS, AND BEAMS

Have you ever connected toy blocks to construct a building? Or created a castle out of cards or a tower out of bricks? With construction toys, the sky is the limit! And the best part? The structures you make can be disassembled and rebuilt again and again.

4

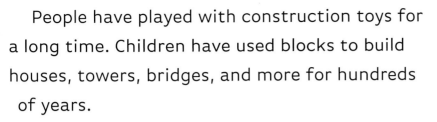

People have played with construction toys for a long time. Children have used blocks to build houses, towers, bridges, and more for hundreds of years.

In the early 1900s, toy companies started making more complicated building toys. ERECTOR sets, Tinker Toys, Lincoln Logs, and LEGOs became very popular. Today, these toys still inspire kids and adults around the world to build amazing toy structures!

MANY MATERIALS

Building toys have been made of many materials throughout history. These include wood, stone, metal, cardboard, resin, and plastic.

MAKING BLOCKS AND CONSTRUCTION SETS

Every day, workers around the world use machinery, tools, and molds to make all kinds of construction toys. Wooden blocks begin with workers hauling lumber to factories. The lumber is measured, sawed, and polished into uniform blocks.

Workers use machines to bend, cut, and mold the metal pieces that come in ERECTOR sets. Special machines craft the small parts to precise measurements. This way, pieces fit together perfectly!

LEGOs are also made to fit together. They begin as huge pieces of plastic. The plastic is melted and squeezed into LEGO-sized metal molds. The pieces are cooled, packaged, and shipped to stores. Then they are ready to be used to build bridges, boats, cars, castles, and more!

MINI LOG CABINS

Lincoln Logs were invented in 1916. They are small wooden logs with notches near each end. The notches can be fit together to construct buildings. Lincoln Logs come in sets that include special pieces for roofs and **chimneys**. Some sets also contain people and animal pieces. Lincoln Logs were added to the US National Toy Hall of Fame in 1999.

BECOME A TOY MAKER

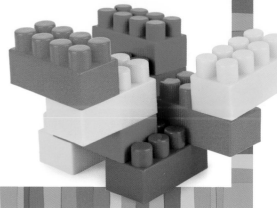

THINK LIKE A TOY MAKER

Present-day blocks come in many different shapes, sizes, and colors. LEGOs are made in many themes. Some ERECTOR sets are robotic. There are also building blocks that light up. Toy makers think of many creative toy features. Then they find ways to make their ideas work in the toys they design.

As you work on the projects in this book, think like a toy maker! Read the steps and look at the photos. Do any pieces

8

inspire you to create different features or structures? Is there a way to improve on a brick's design?

HAVE FUN!

Construction toys are made to inspire creativity and fun. Making these toys should be fun too! Get creative as you do the projects in this book.

You might decide to make the suggested blocks giant-sized or tiny. Or you might come up with a new way to connect the building-block cards. Go for it! Construction toys are all about imagination. Have fun creating your own **versions** of the blocks in this book!

MATERIALS

HERE ARE SOME OF THE MATERIALS YOU'LL NEED FOR THE PROJECTS IN THIS BOOK.

acrylic paint

adhesive hook & loop tape

air-dry clay

card stock

clear casting epoxy kit

craft sticks

crayons

disposable plastic cup

drawstring pouch

face mask

hot glue gun & glue sticks

LEGO baseplates

LEGOs

neodymium
magnets

non-latex
gloves

paintbrush

paper plate

picture
frame

ruler

scissors

silicone ice
cube tray

Some projects in
this book use strong
chemicals or hot
tools. This means
these projects need
adult help. You may
see one or more
safety symbols at
the beginning of a
project. Here is what
they mean:

 HOT

 FACE MASK

 GLOVES

LEGO DESKTOP

TRANSFORM YOUR DESK WITH LEGO ACCESSORIES BUILT BY YOU!

ATTACHING THE BASEPLATES

1 This project includes attaching LEGO baseplates to a desk or table. This may damage the surface. Ask a parent for **permission** before starting.

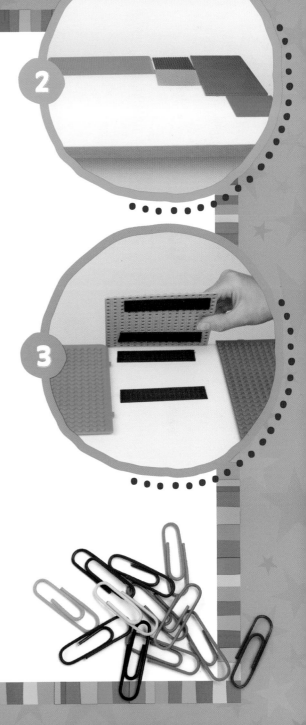

2 Arrange the baseplates around the sides of the desk. Make sure there is enough uncovered space in the middle to draw, write, or do homework.

3 Use the hook and loop tape to attach the baseplates to the desktop. Stick strips of the scratchy side to the desk. Stick strips of the soft side to the backs of the baseplates.

(continued on next page)

MATERIALS
desk or table
LEGO baseplates
adhesive hook & loop tape
paper
LEGOs

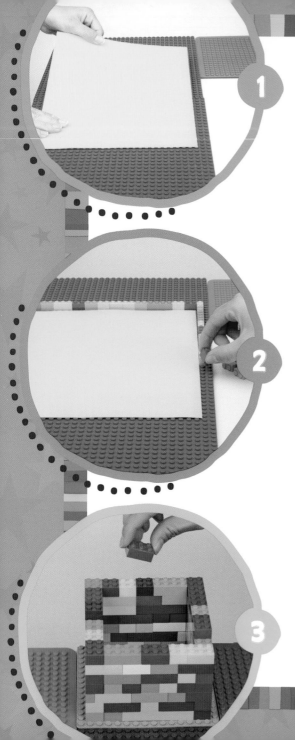

BUILDING ACCESSORIES

1 Build a tray for holding homework and other papers. Lay a piece of paper on a large baseplate.

2 Place narrow LEGOs around three sides of the paper.

3 Use LEGOs to construct a pencil holder. Make a square tower about 14 **studs** long on each side. Build the tower about 11 rows high.

TRY THIS!
*To create a different setup, just rearrange the LEGOs into new **accessories**!*

4 Add a bin to keep extra LEGOs handy. Make the walls about three rows high.

5 Build small bins to hold paper clips or other supplies.

6 Use LEGOs to write short, fun messages or labels.

7 Leave one baseplate empty. You can use the space to build with LEGOs when you need a homework break!

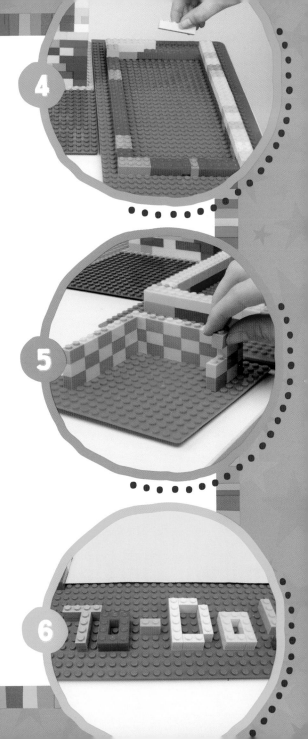

LEGENDARY LEGOS

Have you ever built with LEGOs? More than 400 billion of these little bricks have been made since their creation!

Ole Kirk Christiansen founded the LEGO company in 1932. The company made wooden toys and other products. Fourteen years later, Christiansen bought a plastic-**injection** machine. Christiansen and his employees experimented with the machine.

Three years later, in 1949, the first LEGOs were born! They were plastic bricks with **studs** that **interlock**. As LEGOs became more and more popular, the company developed sets of bricks and

accessories, such as LEGO cars and people. Today, LEGO produces 4,200 different LEGO elements. The pieces come in 58 colors and are sold in stores around the world.

FITTING TOGETHER

LEGOs have been updated over the years. But each and every piece is made to be **compatible** with the others. Bricks and accessories made in the 1950s can be used with ones made today.

MINI MAGNETIC BLOCKS

CRAFT TINY CLAY BLOCKS THAT STICK TOGETHER!

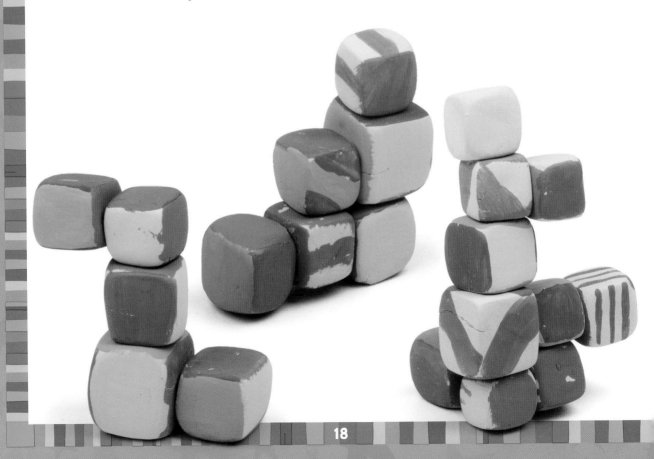

1 Wrap a small piece of air-dry clay around a magnet.

2 Roll the clay into a ball.

3 Set the ball on a flat surface. Use a ruler to press the ball into a cube. Press one side, and then rotate. Keep rotating and pressing until the sides are flat.

(continued on next page)

CAUTION!

The magnets for this project are very strong! Be careful when separating them so your fingers don't get pinched.

MATERIALS

air-dry clay
small neodymium magnets

ruler
paper plate
acrylic paint
paintbrush

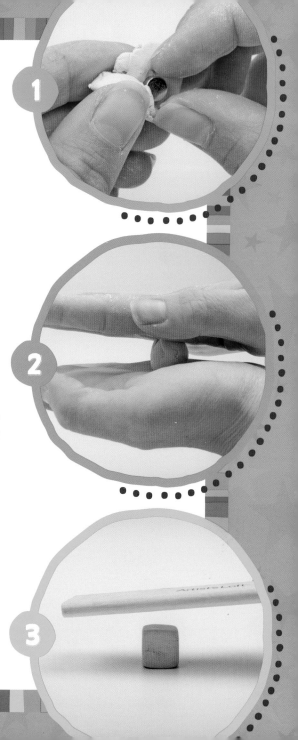

4 Repeat steps 1 through 3 to create more cubes.

5 Let the cubes dry on a paper plate. Set the cubes several inches apart so the magnets inside don't pull the cubes together!

6 When the cubes are dry, paint them fun colors. Let the paint dry.

7 Build cool creations with your magnetic blocks. Try building sculptures on the side of a refrigerator!

TRANSPARENT BLOCKS

MAKE CLEAR BLOCKS CONTAINING GLITTER OR SMALL OBJECTS!

MATERIALS

- silicone ice cube tray
- 8 small disposable plastic cups of the same size
- permanent marker
- face mask
- non-latex gloves
- clear casting epoxy kit
- craft sticks

ITEMS TO EMBED IN THE BLOCKS, SUCH AS:
- buttons
- coins
- game pieces
- glitter
- googly eyes
- marbles
- plastic bugs
- small action figures
- small flowers
- small keys
- small leaves

PREPARING THE MOLDS AND RESIN

1 Decide what items you want to put in your blocks. If any are almost as big as the ice cube tray cups, put them in the cups now. Save smaller items until later.

2 Number four plastic cups 1 through 4. Set the cups in order.

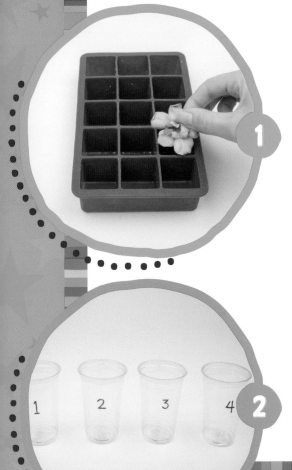

3 Make sure your work area is well-**ventilated**. Put on the face mask and gloves. Remove the resin and hardener from the epoxy kit.

4 Carefully pour resin into cup 1. Fill it almost half full.

5 Carefully pour hardener into cup 2. Fill cup 2 so its contents are level with cup 1.

6 Pour the contents of cups 1 and 2 together into cup 3.

(continued on next page)

PRO TIP!

Cover your work surface with newspaper when mixing and pouring resin. Spills and drips can harden and ruin surfaces.

7 Slowly stir cup 3 for 2 minutes with a craft stick. Make sure to scrape the sides and bottom of the cup.

8 Pour the mixture from cup 3 into cup 4.

9 Use another craft stick to slowly stir cup 4 for 2 minutes.

POURING AND SETTING

1 Pour the resin mixture into the ice cube tray. Fill empty cups almost halfway. Fill any cups that contain items to the top.

2 If there are bubbles, carefully stir or poke the resin surface with a new craft stick. If you want glitter in your blocks, add it now.

3 Let the resin harden for 24 hours. Place the small items on top of the resin in the half-full cups.

4 Repeat steps 2 through 9 on pages 22 through 24. Use new cups and stir sticks. Fill the half-full cups to the top. Add more glitter if you want.

5 Let the resin harden for 24 hours. Pop the blocks out of the molds. Use them to create cool, see-through structures!

JUMBO 2-D BRICKS

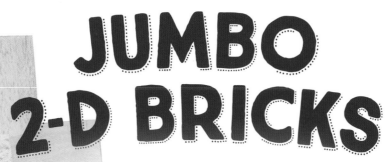

CREATE AND CONNECT HUGE CARDS TO CONSTRUCT CASTLES, BUILDINGS, BRIDGES, AND MORE!

MATERIALS

card stock
scissors
marker
ruler
crayons,
   colored
   pencils, or
   markers

1 Cut a large rectangle out of card stock. Use the rectangle to trace as many rectangles as you want. Cut the rectangles out.

2 On each rectangle, make marks 1 inch (2.5 cm) from each corner on the long sides. Cut a small slit on each mark.

3 Color and decorate your card blocks.

4 Build structures by tucking the cards' slits into each other. Have fun and be creative!

TRY THIS!

Turn any leftover card stock strips or pieces into blocks too. Cut small slits near their corners, as in step 2.

3-D LEGO MURAL

BUILD A HANGING LEGO BASE, AND CREATE A 3-D MASTERPIECE!

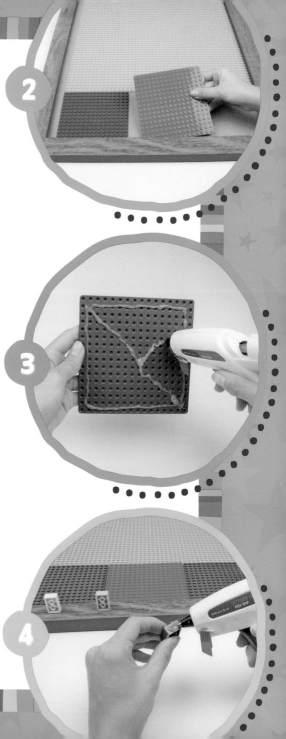

1 If you are using a picture frame, remove the glass and reassemble the backing onto the frame.

2 Lay the frame or bulletin board on a flat surface. Arrange LEGO baseplates inside the border.

3 Hot glue the LEGO baseplates in place.

4 Hot glue several LEGO pieces along the bottom edge of the frame. These will be used as pegs.

(continued on next page)

MATERIALS

bulletin board or large picture frame

LEGO baseplates

hot glue gun & glue sticks

LEGOs

small drawstring pouches

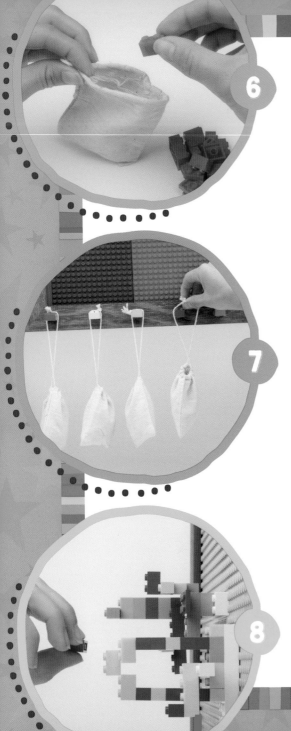

5 Let the glue dry. Then hang the frame on a wall.

6 Put LEGOs in the drawstring pouches.

7 Hang the pouches from the LEGO pegs.

8 Use the LEGOs to construct a 3-D **mural**. Remove and rearrange the LEGOs whenever you want a new mural!

TRY THIS!

Build **shelves** out of LEGOs on your mural. Then use the shelves to display other LEGO creations!

GLOSSARY

accessory – something that is not necessary but makes something else more useful, attractive, or effective.

chimney – a hollow pipe or other structure on a roof that smoke comes out of.

compatible – able to be used with another device or system without making changes.

inject – to forcefully introduce a substance into something.

interlock – to attach by putting one part inside another.

mini – short for miniature. A small copy or model of something.

mural – a picture painted on a wall or a ceiling.

permission – when a person in charge says it is okay to do something.

shelf – a thin, flat surface used to store things.

stud – a small raised area on the surface of something.

ventilated – having fresh air moving through.

version – a different form or type from the original.

WEBSITES

To learn more about Cool Toys & Games, visit **booklinks.abdopublishing.com**. These links are routinely monitored and updated to provide the most current information available.

INDEX